Lighting the Furnace Pilot

Paul Ruffin

Spoon River Poetry Press
P. O. Box 1443
Peoria, Illinois
61655

Poems in this collection have previously appeared in the following magazines: *Southwest Heritage, Quartet, Texas Quarterly, Barataria Review, Green River Review, Kansas Quarterly, New England Review, Texas Prize Stories and Poems, The Little Review, Quarterly West, New Mexico Humanities Review, Mississippi Valley Review, Georgia Review, California Quarterly, Descant, Roanoke Review, Mississippi Review, New River Review, New South Anthology, Old Hickory Review, Wascana Review, Natchez Trace Review, Michigan Quarterly Review,* and *University of Tampa Review.*

Printed by D.J. Graphics, Peoria.
Cover by Suan Guess-Welcker, Bloomington, Illinois
ISBN: 0-933180-08-X
Library of Congress Number: 80-50012

for Sharon

The Dream

Grandma Arnold

Lighting the Furnace Pilot

Lighting the Furnace Pilot

Cold must come hard to our hill
these winter nights, drive my wife
to wool, her mood to ice,
before I will climb to the attic
to light the furnace pilot.
There are no skeletons in my loft,
no pulsing bats; a firm mind
and wire mesh keep them out
with the early frost and ruined leaves:
It is neither fate nor fear.
My ascension creaks the ladder
and I slide back the panel and
hoist my extra twenty pounds
up among the rafters.
No bats, or bones, I think,
my fingers finding the knob
that will put breath back
into this winter house.
Then the blue jet sings,
fire pops from a hundred holes
as I hunker in the dark and warm
my hands on the furnace sides.
Above my head the leaves
flit and finger across the roof
and the wind, heavier and a year
older, moans from fate or fear.

Cleaning the Well

Each spring there was the well to be cleaned.
On a day my grandfather would say,
"It's got to be done. Let's go." This time
I dropped bat and glove, submitted to the rope,
and he lowered me into the dark and cold
water of the well. The sun
slid off at a crazy cant and I
was there, thirty feet down, waist deep
in icy water, grappling for whatever
was not pure and wet and cold.
The sky hovered like some pale moon
above, eclipsed by his heavy red face
bellowing down to me not to dally,
to feel deep and load the bucket.
My feet rasped against cold stone,
toes selecting unnatural shapes, curling
and gripping, raising them to my fingers,
then into the bucket and up to him:
a rubber ball, pine cones, leather glove,
beer can, fruit jars, an indefinable bone.
It was a time of fears: suppose he
should die or forget me, the rope break,
the water rise, a snake strike, the
bottom give way, the slick sides crumble?

The last bucket filled, my grandfather
assured, the rope loop dropped to me
and I was delivered by him who
sent me down, drawn slowly to sun
and sky and his fiercely grinning face.
"There was something else down there:
a cat or possom skeleton, but it
broke up, I couldn't pick it up."

4

He dropped his yellow hand on my head.
"There's always something down there
you can't guite get in your hands.
You'd know that if it wasn't your first
trip down. You'll know from now on."

"But what about the water?
Can we keep on drinking it?"

"You've drunk all that cat
you're likely to drink. Forget it
and don't tell the others. It's just
one more secret you got to live with."

The Graffittist

A self-called antiChrist,
He sits in silence
Behind the bolted door, the freshly
Greened walls a warm new world
For his Word.

I turn the faucet off, listen
With wet hands for the hiss
Of felt-tip, the low laugh as he
Looks on his message.

I slip into the hall,
Content not to see those yellow eyes,
The cold, triangular head:
I need no face to teach me dread.
There are always words and walls.

The Hitchhiker and the Fat Woman

This room, sour with your bulk,
fills with the juices of life,
fecund and inexorable: real
beyond shadows of the morning sun
inching across your kitchen floor.

Nearly teethless, lacking a finger
on your left hand, you ferry a platter
of eggs and baloney to me, a face
from off the highway, a face that must
be fed. You fret that your dress
is unfit for company, your house a mess,
no bacon or ham in the icebox.
I eat the eggs and scabby baloney
and hold my breath against your strength.

You talk of family and dead husband,
wring your hands in your apron front
and look away out the window. I say
nothing, scrape back my chair, nod
and head back to the highway. You wave
from the porch, a vague bladder
of flesh against the dark doorway.

I have tried to rid my mind of you,
old woman, stuck there: a bad poem
which will not declare itself
or one which simply will not end.
It is years now since you waved
from that doorway, yet troubled nights
before or between sags of sleep
you heave up like an overripe moon
and smother me with your light.

A Sign in April

The road to the sanitorium
cuts off the interstate,
lingers by someone's front yard,
then turns back into a line of trees
beyond which I cannot see.
I see it, going,
the road that loses itself
in the trees where leaves
have just turned green.

This cough I've had, this
cough doubtless draws me
to look for the sign, small
green sign saying
            SANITORIUM
in white letters, a simple sign.

This cough, tightness in there,
turns me to it; just around
a certain bend in the interstate
and I have to look at it,
swivel my head to the road
and follow it off into the trees
where a white water tower
rises like a cough mushroomed
into bright air a cold morning,
a silent cough I can't recall
until the sign stands
green and simple from the shoulder
and points to the turn where
a gravel road leads off past a yard
with a white fence, mailbox,
flowers by a walk.

Deep-Sea Fishing

In farm ponds or rivers
there is always the bottom
to be felt, something at the end
of your paddle or pole
to tell you the earth is there;

and the longest gar
is less than the length of your leg;
fish with two eyes, one on a side,
look right, even in air, scales
or skin familiar as freckles.

But here the terrible fish feed deep,
huddling around sand-choked ships,
whatever lies below: pipelines, abandoned nets,
the one-eyed, grotesque, colors
and shapes of another world.
Here hauling in a taken line
is done with care, a club
close by, a sharp knife
to cut the singing line.
The cottonmouth, the
thunder-jawed loggerhead, the sharp-
toothed gar are petty thoughts
here where the fish feed deep
and silent and their unknown forms
run deep behind the eyes.

It is like the fear of falling,
here where the earth fails us;
and even when the old known sun
has flattened out the sea
like a hammer on lead,
as the line goes slicing,
fingers tighten on the rod,
eyes tighten on the sea,
the deep, dark green of the sea.

Death at the "Y"

It should not matter,
when the old heart stops,
whether it happens at home
in bed, in a bus full of
people, or—God forbid—
here at the "Y."

But we all have quiet fears:
laughing out loud in church,
flatulence in class—
some probable impossibility
that makes cowards of us all.
I would like most
not to die at the "Y":
On the court, one final
sag to the floor, boy-smudged
basketballs gathered in a corner
to witness, my hand-ball mate
wide-eyed, gloved hands at his sides
like old men's balls;
or in the dressing room, the sting
of man-sweat driving
my breath
deeper, one
flash
of hairy legs;
not here, where even the secretary
carries her arms like parentheses.

I ask little, only a last
impression somewhere not at the "Y":
a girl's laugh, smooth legs,
round little female ass
yo-yoing off into whatever dark.

Calf in an Abandoned Well

Once more those images storm my mind
this day of sun and easy air;
once more black wings spiral down,
whoom to a stop beside the hole.
And dark settles on the land, chokes
the summer hill wind, stills the eyes
like farm ponds before the blackness breaks.

The shaping of an afternoon is slow.
The pines opened like a wound
and then the well was there, around
it dark birds, horny heads
bobbing, the shuffling mass whirling
like pagans in some fierce dance.
They broke in a clap of bright black,
rose into the trees, arching them
with dark wind, and the calf
belly glowed from the well bottom,
pinioned by a shaft of stench.

The years have driven us our ways:
bright hours and dark, your letters coming
fewer, less often, saying less, lost
deep in whatever wounds we have left.
I cannot say what ties us yet,
perhaps nothing, perhaps the tenuous
clutch we still have: the sense of black,
unfathomable black: well and wing,
the sag of a summer afternoon
into Orphic loss, some dark wind.

The Blue Balloon

Look, the balloon, the climb
    toward orange-
    fringed western clouds,
    the blue dot rising.
Look the balloon is gone:
    your hand loosened, the string
    pulled through; we will
    get another another day.
The break there between tall clouds
    opens like bruised jaws bloody
    with rising through rough earth.
It is going into the clouds, there;
    follow my finger, there
    where the two big clouds
    are coming together.
He cannot see where my finger points
    into thick evening clouds,
    and the balloon is gone.
It is not worth looking back for,
    there will be others,
    I promise as the dark
    closes now like earth-bruised jaws
    on the child tugging away at my hand.

My Dog Stares

My dog stares
as I slip a bottle from the car;
he will not tell,
never has,
as if he knows
whatever ghost I rage against
is his as well as mine
and somehow the bottle helps.

He will grumble through the night
at shadows on the road
whether he knows them or not,
suspicion his nature,
and I, wise with wine,
will fondle the shadowy hands of night
and growling wake to a mindful of bones.

On Being in Love and Finding It Impossible to Study French Poetry

I cannot touch Baudelaire's flame:
Words go around
but the images will not stay,
cast in bronzed smoke;
they crack and splinter
and words fall aclatter.
What's cold sings
like slender stone.

This Instamatic Magic
(To Scott)

This Instamatic magic that is you,
    you beneath the peachtree,
    hands full of red fruit
    and beside you a dog:
Conceived in a flick,
    you, the dog, a peachtree with peaches,
    you waited in dark after white light
    found you, waited
and came floating up out of
    black water
    into the green and red world
    I hold flat in my palm:
you, my lost son, a handful of peaches,
    and a dog.

Divorce

The word slides easy
off the tongue
like ice sloughing
off a window in winter
when the sun burns through:
little trinkets of hard light
that slice into the black
behind the eyes
until corners melt
and the light lies soft and dumb.

Night on I-59

Back there
    a dozen feet behind me
    rides all of what I own,
    a trailer full of books;
and we head south into
    a belly of stars
    and O Lord not one
    bright enough to follow:
little night-turned, tossed
    tits
    hanging up there,
    dragging through
    sloughs along the road;
and O Lord, dangle me one
    I can burn my mouth on,
one firm mouthful to
    suck and chew on
    until the sky breaks through
    to a warm milk dawn.

English Class in the Animal Husbandry Building

That certain time of year
when the air blue-needle keen
pricks away what leaves remain
outside this third-floor window,
below they shine their tools
to slaughter the pigs
whose grunts we hear
above our classroom noises.

Knowing those hot knives down there
turns my mind from words
but I stumble on until
squeals strike through my bluff
and I dismiss the class,
those hog-killing days
when blue air bites
and sun slits the eyes like steel.

The Dream

The Dream

She leached to him like a hagfish
for twenty-eight years
until the blue he saw was
the same blue to her
and they dreamed the same dream:
a redwood cabin, a lake,
a dog by the door.

Then the job went sour,
years of welding with the same torch,
laying the seams as easy and straight
as the rows they dreamed of corn
and beans beside the lake
and cabin, the dog by the door;

went sour and the blue they saw
was not the same, the soil
of their dreams grown sour,
the corn and beans rotted
beside the stale lake
and fallen cabin door
where a lean dog whines
and scuffs at his sores.

Hotel Fire: New Orleans

From first light we fear falling:
after the fever of birth, impetus
toward that natural window, we
reach, cling, our fingers and toes
curled to grip, after the fire
that tempers us for the sun.

There I saw them—I see them still—
thrust from windows,
flailing like children
who know the earth has failed them:
they snatch at chinks, to ledges,
tumble to the wet street below,
the fire an old and certain death,
the leap the only faith that's left.

After the Fire at the Old Folks Home

Deep in this smoke-choked night
they line the armory hall
like frightened children: clutching
a purse here, a blanket there,
pictures and paper sacks.
The shock-stained faces so soon
jarred from sleep hold the long stare
of dream, the slow motion of dream.
Fingers tighten whitely on the
few salvaged scraps of lives
while we wipe away smudges
and bandage what bleeds or burns.
And then we leave them, dumb
to say it will be better tomorrow,
the sun will come, the night go.
What child or bird could rise
renewed with bright eyes shining
after such an ashy death,
so fierce a night of burning?

To a Student on the Front Row

Children may someday
pick up your bones, a late
April, from the secret earth,
feel your fingers the way
I roll this piece of chalk; your
pelvic bone scrubbed clean
of mud and moss,
turned up on a log,
the girlflesh gone, the bright
hair, that bleached chamber hollow
to the rattle of stones they toss;
your smooth thigh
bones, in their hot hands,
will bludgeon frogs and snakes,
and teeth I have dreamed against
mine will be parceled out
among small pockets
to clack with marbles and rocks.
On the front row, on the front
your hair lies across your
shoulders, soft and warm
in a yellow rib of sun.

To Patsy: Tenth Grade

You were as common those days,
Patsy, as a squat milk jug,
dress tugged to cover your ankles,
lipstick as taboo as beer,
and so swollen on Christ
we took your word
when you said He was your lover.

But when Vandevender took you
back there behind the gym
in those tall dark weeds
and you gave up the ghost,
your resurrected bones
turned the world round for us
who saw you rise from damp rushes
that night like a silver chalice
rubbed bright by the master's hands.

Incontinence Was the Word

Incontinence was the word that hung
in my throat when I told my wife: He
cannot control bowels, bladder, anything.

But from the den window where she could see
the new black kitten laying out
his world, she would not believe: He

seems so right, she said, so as he ought
to be—we could try a week, two, three,
give him a chance, some sort of fight.

Then flies came, late in the first week,
green/gold flies latched to his hind legs
sopped with urine; and sleep

itself was no mercy, the injected eggs
festering anal tissues, the hellish flies
boring into flesh and outraging

kitten dreams. At last he tried
only to forget, hunched in a tight knot,
exposing nothing, refusing water and food.

This morning he is safe from the clot
of flies on his bed. Boxed like a gift
for a pretty lady, he does not

move, does not cry for relief,
food, or the freedom of the backyard;
he is, we think, beyond kitten belief

in what he thought we could provide,
and does know that even we cannot control
at times what we try and ought to hide.

Female Cousins at Thanksgiving

The old Thanksgiving game
    has brought them to the country
    to Grandma's house,
    the full table
    and ageless talk of ageless aunts
    and uncles and things
    that used to be.
Boys ring the woods
    with man sound, their
    long shadows knifing the fields
    for rabbits and birds, their
    guns rolling the hills
    with rhythms of the hunt,
    the dance of young gods.
From the smokey, too-hot house
    the girls slip
    to loiter in the sun
    at the edge of the back porch;
    a radio tinkles between them,
    the fields lie before them,
    and then the woods and hills,
    the smoky distant shapes of boys.
Talk goes round in the thick room,
    the television shows a ballgame,
    bellies and memories are full;
But lean boys slip
    through the woods, intent
    on grey ghosts
While the girls huddle outside,
    whisper and giggle
    and wait for a glimpse of the gods.

To a Child Putting Together a Puzzle: *Prairie Pursuit*

Child, if the brown swirl of hair
    refuses to fit the face
red in frostlight there
    and the tiny withered trace
of a nose defies
    a smooth-fingered fit
somewhere between the eyes
    and brows of it,
do not force the mesh;
    the human will,
shrouded with flesh,
    will linger still
in the form it knows,
    rough-edged and rare,
patterned in the grace of fear.

She is running, we see
    by the picture on the box,
across the ripe-wheat sea
    toward the white rocks
where a trail of smoke lies flat
    on the winter morning sky
and the grayboard leaning shack
    swings its door wide
to take her in, in from cold
    and leatherfooted marauders
who leap even now, hot and bold
    in the thin tall grain behind her.

Bigfoot Expedition

It was a mad hippy,
      they said, who came
down to their camp
      from the high hills
to tell them a tale of Bigfoot.

We were there with reels
of film and bags of plaster
for casts of those big feet,
all with degrees and years
of exploding myths behind us.
And we found nothing, nothing.
      "He came like a bright blue shadow
      down a snow ledge, crouched
      by my tent and whispered:
      it sounded like crushed stones."

There were no tracks, no spoor,
no broken branches, nothing.
      "Like heavy stones grinding together
      while he crouched beside my tent."

So we wrote it off as drugs,
packed back down to the main camp
and turned to more solid things.

Under the high hills moon
      a shaggy blue shadow
pads the snow slope down
      to an orange tent, crouches,
and the air is filled
      with the sound of crumbling stone.

The High-School English Teacher Retires

For thirty-five years
   she did battle
against ignorance,
   that childhood evil:
nurtured the wise,
   subdued the rabble,
and wrestled with all
   the certain uncertainties
that scar even the soul.

At sixty she simply
   wound down
   like a childless toy:
shelved her books, turned
   once around
   in the chalky room
   and tilted on home.

She says she is beyond hurt
   now, even the recent wounds
   do not matter at this age
and the old ones lie smooth
   as frozen lakes at dawn.

Earl Maguerny's Boat

When Earl Maguerny said one day
he believed he'd build a boat,
Cora nodded sure you will
and dreamed it four-feet long
and fit for a mantle.

When reclaimed lumber filled
their lot and the suburb
folk stopped to smile and point,
she knew he meant a *boat*.

And over the months the bottom beam,
laid forty-feet straight, fleshened
into bright ribs, then darkened
under heavy planks while
neighbors pointed, smiled,
and called it a damned sight.

Soon for miles around the great
gray ark was all they talked about:
Sundays the cars would pass and stop
and kids would yell "Noah! Noah!"
and all would cackle and move on—
and many the night Earl would
crawl down into the glare
of someone's headlights from the street.
Still on he worked and the masts rose
and caulking shone like veins along
the deep sweep of the sides.

When one day the family came
and asked just what the deuce he meant,
he answered: "I'm building a boat."
"But people are talking, Grandad,
the neighbors think you're daft."
"May be, but I'm gonna build my boat,
and when the time comes me
and Cora are gonna sail it
all around the world, here to there,
and maybe twice if we want to."

For years the gray bulk sat
in the corner of Earl and Cora's yard,
flowing with the sun and ebbing
with the dark, the three masts
like white crosses rising with dawn.

Then the old man's strength went
and his ship that danced so high
and dry foundered in suburban seas:
the masts leaned, seams split.
And when the family safely dropped
him into the ground in a metal canoe
with fond words and thanks to the Lord
sons-in-laws reclaimed the boat
to the earth, nail by nail
and board by board.

Pompeii

In the glare of the day the tragic
shape will not come: colorful
tourists clatter about the streets
and the ruins reflect civic
concern: the high polish of trade.
The ash has been scooped, buried,
blown away to bare this bright
place to common air, the sun,
and busy prying hands and eyes.
Ah, the tragedy lacks its starch,
wilts in this bustle and chatter.

Here on the night slopes of Vesuvius
the tragic tale begins: Pompeii
rises from the ash-dark plain, the moon
coaxes inch by inch walls and columns.
Dogs bark, the earth moves,
bent and broken rise and walk,
the scorched, the stifled—all
bright and whole in the moon's healing.

But the sun wakes what the moon dreams.
Its first slashes bring the color back,
vehicles move, a slow string of early
tourists inches toward the town.
The ghosts are gone, the tragedy still.
Polished ruins sit waiting
vacant on the dawning plain.

Wyeth's "Winter Fields"

The crow is appropriately black
and appropriately dead
in the foreground of these winter fields;
the sky lies like fallow steel
and the fields no longer try,
rust-smeared across a cold world
where a crow falls without
catching that ancient eye.

Wyeth's "Distant Thunder"

Beyond her hill under the white sky
shards of bone lie in red sand
and paunchy old men lean from
carriages, focus their glasses
on the trembling plains,
smile and say their words;
but the stain of blueberries
purples her lips, their smell
lies heavy on her hands,
and she has watched nothing but birds.

The Practice Is Over, Tom Hardy

When you are turned this time
from your worm-drilled coffins, ghosts,
it will not be the thump of guns,
the firefly practice on the coast.

The shudder that shakes
the Salisbury Plain,
the hot press of shock,
will spare the glebe cow pain
and instant-fleece the flock,
leaving a sooty shadow
where the hound had lain.

It will be warmer then indeed:
the Judgment will be known at last,
when Stourton Tower poofs like Camelot
and Stonehenge melts like glass.

To the Twenty-first Century

Blue-clad boy
asleep under the haystack
or lost in the corn,
drag out and blow again
your old and tarnished horn,
now that the cows have bloated
and the sheep run wild;
blow it again,
now that the order we held
as fine-balanced and fragile
as a house of straws
has tumbled to the wind;
blow it again, you first
notion that order does not last,
blue innocent in a book
of color and rhymes where
there is no future nor past.
Up and blow, boy, blow to
the skies, but know that your
tune is lost on casual green and blue;
as you wish, stand and blow,
though bronze to iron to atom
to dreamless sleep is the way
that this story will go.

Grandma Arnold

Circle and Stone

For Amelia Gray, a wept-away week
after the shock of the jilting,
the silk dress folded, laid back
in a closet with pressed flowers;

but for this wedding day gone sour
he has felt no grief, a thousand
miles away from her encircling arms.
The shadow of the bus tumbles
across rows of early corn and he
slumps back into sleep.

Her pale fingers return the ring
to its velvet case, and the stone
glints up to her like broken glass
throwing back the sun.

While he rides west away
from the circle and stone.

But empress and clown must turn
deep hours to the sacrament of dream,
their flesh secure in stone:
only fierce dream, annealed and pure
absorbs the shock of blood.
So sweet Amelia lies beneath
her down and lace, her face
a calm review of death.
Night turns round outside her open window
and the stone sky cracks a slender glow.

Rebound

She married Grandpa on the rebound,
coming back off a hurt hot as fever:
I was a ball those days, she said,
coulda bounced forever and ever—
But your mama needed to be born
and John had to have a farm and wife,
so I shelved my bounce with peaches and beans
and actually felt a kind of relief
it was over. But nothing's ever over
when what you fight is round as a ball
and bounces back and turns you forever
from its center and you as weak and small
as a gnat on an orange. No wonder
he finally got enough. I'd have joined him
in the barn that day if I had only known
that he had got to the center of things;
but he beat me there and would not tell
me, tight as a knot those last few years.
So I bounced right back from his small hell
and aimed myself at the stars.

The Hill

I

That stormy pair
never took advice:
bought the hard hill
and chopped out a farm,
the two of them fierce,
stiff as saddles,
breaking in the land;
and the springs crawled by,
mule drawn, blushing
with green the hillback
under the bellies of storms.

The Church

To her the church was not a white
steepled thing of distant sacred wood
but a sprawling live oak
in the middle of a harsh field—
When back-ache and heat
and gritty teeth wore her to her knees
she'd go there, lean into cool bark
until her soul knew full release
and took on the primal power of that dark
wood, transformed to some light and holy thing
with halo and robe and wings.

The Hill

II

It is not dirt to him;
that dearth of loam
sheeting the gray ridge;
he has watched it thread
away in the rain,
seeking a surer base
when contour rows
and walls of stone
would not last
after the crack of frost.

Sunday

Sunday is for rest, she told him,
time for leaning back and loving—
and going off to church.
She showed him in the Book.

"Just another day for weeds
to creep in," he returned,
"they don't rest on Sunday,"
and went on hoing while she
sat on the steps and watched.

That night she turned to him:
"God comes down hard on them
that denies his word."

"Then let the Lord tell them weeds
to take a day off and go fishing
or to church, just quit growing
one day; then I'll drop my hoe,
dress in my very best, and go
wherever you say. But until
they stop crowding in, this hill
can't stand no day of rest."

So with her face knotted like a fist
she turned back to her Bible
while he slid into a still
Sunday of weedless green fields.

The Hill
III

The snap, rafter groan,
slow spin in cracklight,
he hangs
until she finds him there:
blue-blown face a storm
in the corner of a stall;
then, hands at the tight knot,
she drops him to the straw,
eyes on nothing,
pale and cold as frost.

Dark Angel

The storm fell like a sodden
black angel
across the back of the hill
and rode out the night there,
spurring fire on the stones
of the fields, lashing clay flanks
until morning.

The farm lay in the early sun
gray and broken, a damp sag
in the ridge—an old saddle of sin
where the dark angel had been.

The Hill

IV

On a slab
the frame of a cat:
chapel of bone,
smooth symmetry of white ribs,
polish of rain and frost
on bone and stone
keeping off the moss;
cat cage and no cat,
light cracks in and light cracks out,
the out and in of it
tinkling in her head
at this hardpan of the dead.

Those Nights

She could stand the taxes:
there was money enough for that;
she was strong as an ox
and kept the house and barn tight
against the wind and rain.
What hammered the door those nights
with a sharper fist than hail
brought the outrageous pain.

With the yellow-haired child
asleep and warm in the back room
she slumped before the graying fire,
sat with herself while the door
rattled like a maddened drum
with the hollow knock and distant call
of nothing, nothing, nothing at all.

Grandma Looks at the Moon

If they have walked up there
you sure can't tell it from here—
Looks the same to me, shines
    the same.

Rockets don't carry that far:
They always come right back
to the ground, curl back like
the sky don't want them
poking around up there.
Remember all them skyrockets
y'all used to shoot, the way
they'd swoosh up and go black
like they'd gone on forever
in the night sky . . . .
But you'd always find them
somewhere over in a field
or on top of the barn,
burned out and cold.

The sky won't have it,
man poking his fingers up there
in God's great big eye.
God's got humor, true enough;
a mote or two don't matter;
but folks are getting mighty big
talking about the moon and Mars
like they was to be railway stops.

Rockets to the moon, pshaw!
All done in Hollywood studios
like the movies. But they'll
keep trying, I'm sure, sending
them rockets up, tempting God
to say, "All right—enough's enough."
And whether it's with fire or flood
this time, he'll shut that
great big eye for good.

Grandma Arnold and the Bomb

We never built the prescribed retreat
of concrete and steel, but the fever
was real on our suburban street
and we felt the Judgment was near.
When first the word came down to us
of the Bomb and doom, we took their advice
and stocked for two weeks, enough
water, food, and supplies to survive.

Grandma, we said, now what'll you do
when the Bomb falls and fries us all,
when the rivers are gone with a big achoo
and we're sent well done to hell?
"There ain't no bomb can dry up a river,
ain't no fire at all can send *me* to hell—
I've rode out storms in that ol' cellar
worse than anything that can fall
from an airplane; and even if they
tear up my crops and poison the pond,
the cellar's got food from four years away
good as the day it was canned.
No kind of bomb can scare me like God
when he turns his thunder loose, I'm bound—
My shelter's tight, I'm strong in the Lord,
and my water's from deep in the ground."

Grandma Arnold: Night Storm

Those dead summer nights
when half the stars are blotted out
she watches lightning run the hills
and listens to far, deep thunder.

We really should go to the cellar,
she says: it is a big cloud
coming this way; there may
be high wind and hail.
(But who has time for storms
when the t. v. comes in clear?)
You would sit there around that set
and let the wind take me and the whole
place off and never blink
an eye, she says, and they
grin and nod and think
her merely odd and old.

The wind gathers in the dark,
far bank, the whole sky shrills
while her shadow grows
like a god on the screen
and she waits for a word from the hills.

Grandpa's Picture

If the picture ever moved at all
there was no way we could tell:
the dust seemed just as thick
one year as the next
and Grandma never mentioned it;
so when one day a misthrown ball
caught a corner, spun the old frame
to the floor, we were appalled
at the sound she made and the flame
that rose in her face to burn
away the face that we had known.

No glass was broke and the frame was secure
when she placed it back on the desk,
but we never again were quite sure
of the meaning of the untouched dust
that coated his ancient sepia face
nor the unseen certain hand
that kept it in its place.

The Rolling Store

It came,
his grandmother reported,
as regular as Sunday service,
grinding up the gravel slope
to her mailbox:
"White as Easter and
long as the arm of God!"
And there on shelves
high as a tall man's head
lay trays of butter, sacks
of beans, printed cloth,
soap, nails, jugs of kerosene:
"All a body could pray for."

Asphalt lies to the mailbox now.
("The ride to the grave will be
quick and smooth," he had heard her say.)
Her kitchen stinks of disuse
and roaches haunt her shelves
where a few jars of beans and peaches
squat in dust.
("A body just don't need much any more.")

On a hillside two hollows over,
when the air is right and the
leaves are gone, he can see
from the porch the rusty rolling store
lying on its side like a brown severed arm
in a glacier of grass.

Grandma Chooses Grandpa's Stone

It seems almost absurd to be
putting up this stone after so many years;
looks like a Cadillac beside a nigger shack:
so slick it mirrors, so smooth not even
frost will stick to it. And lord, his slab
cracked and stained and sagging at one end.
Still, he woulda wanted it, so here it is.
It'll never look this good again, so y'all
gather round and let's have a picture.
Be sure you get the saying in—cost enough
to have it carved there and not but part true:
>   Life for him was never very good
>   But he kept on awhile
>   And done the best he could.

Grandma Chooses Her Plot at the County Cemetery

If it can't be out on the hill somewhere
I guess it'll have to be here.
I don't expect where really matters,
only not next to him, not close:
life was too hard for him,
he's soured the soil. Over by
that leaning oak would do, though
the shade won't count—sun, shade,
and shower won't matter then—
and digging them roots'll be hard.
Fine, I want them to suffer putting me down.
And you can find me better next to it,
if you've a mind to come here again
after I'm under and the hill's gone.
And I don't care what you say: you'll
sell that farm and never go back.
It never was nothing to any of you.
By that leaning oak will be just fine;
and make my box simply and cheap,
pine or gum if you can get it, never
liked them shiny steel things: God can't
get to you and you can't get out.
When he splits the sky with the judgment sound,
I want the busting out easy. I want
the coming up easier than the going down.